Email: targetingtriumph@gmail.com

Thank you! Please leave a review, comment, and suggestion to improve our products.

Copyright ©2020

All rights reserved. No part of the publication may be reproduced, stored in a retrieval system, or transmitted in any form or by any means, electronic, mechanical, photocopying, recording or otherwise, without the prior written permission of the publisher.

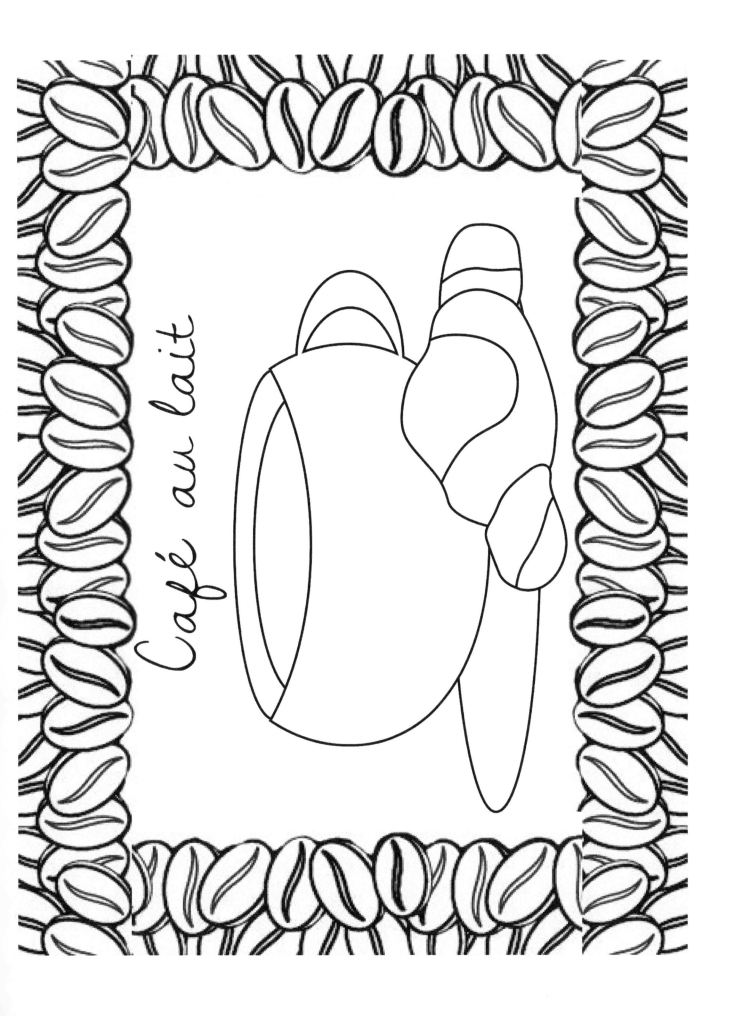

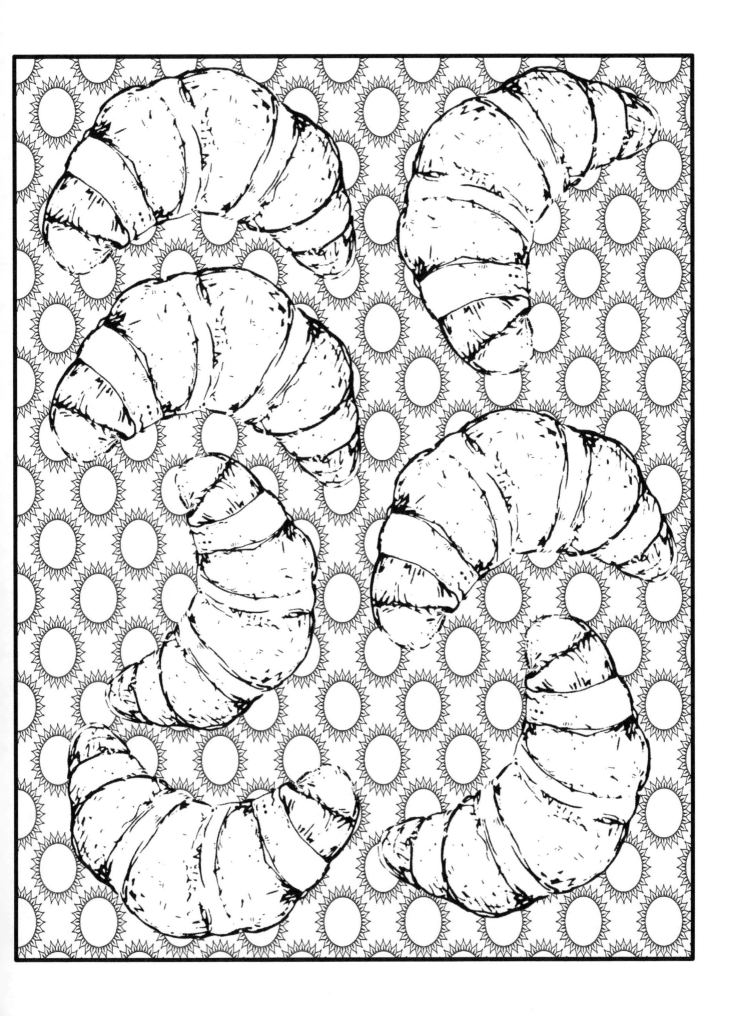

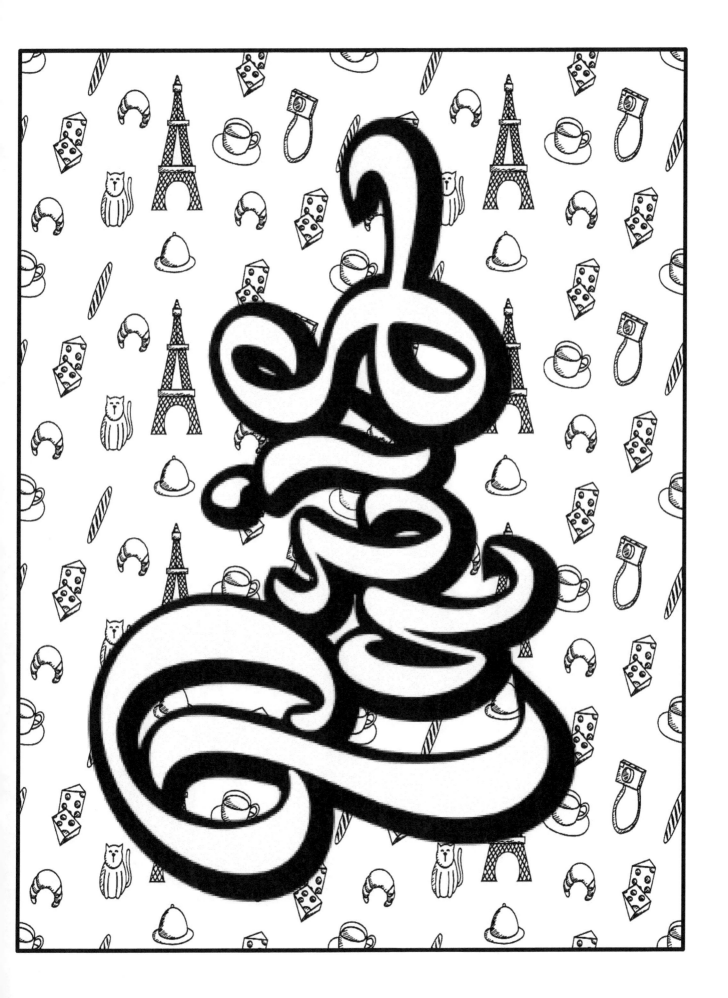